Animal Myths

by Mary Holland

Myth: Porcupines Shoot Their Quills

Porcupines can't run very fast. The only protection they have are special hairs called quills.

Quills are hollow. The tips are sharp and covered with tiny hooks. If they are scared, porcupines tuck in their head, stick out their quills, and look like a big pin cushion.

You may have heard that porcupines can shoot their quills. This is not true. But if an animal touches a porcupine, the quills will become stuck in the animal's skin.

Myth: Skunks Spray Right Away When Scared

Lots of people are scared of striped skunks because they worry skunks will spray them. Skunks only spray if they are very frightened. Even then they give lots of warning. The first thing they do if they are scared is hiss and raise their tail up and over their back. Next, they stamp their front feet on the ground. If you don't go away, they will turn their body in a U-shape so that both their head and their bottom are facing you. If you keep coming closer, you may get sprayed!

Don't try holding a skunk by its tail—it can still spray you!

Myth: Blind as a Bat

Bats are not blind! They have eyes and can see very well. However, to find insects to eat, they depend on their ears more than their eyes.

Bats make a high-pitched sound which bounces off insects and back to the bat. That tells the bat exactly where the insects are, even if it's pitch black. This way of finding something is called echolocation.

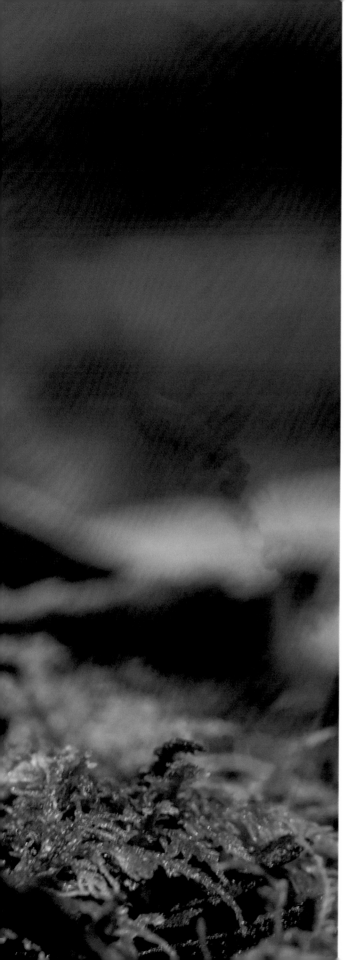

Myth: Touching a Toad Gives You Warts

Holding a toad in your hands will not make you sick or give you warts!

Toads are covered with bumps. Inside some of these bumps, or glands, is a poisonous liquid that would make you sick if you ate the toad.

Toads use the poison to protect themselves from snakes and other animals that might want to eat them (predators). If a dog picks up a toad in its mouth, the dog will start foaming at the mouth and will drop the toad right away.

While you won't get warts if you hold a toad, it might pee on you!

Myth: Dragonflies Sew Mouths Shut or Sting

Dragonflies can fly but they are not dragons!

Because dragonflies are long and thin and look a bit like a sewing needle, people used to believe that they could sew your mouth, ears, or lips shut while you were sleeping. And some people think dragonflies sting.

Dragonflies cannot sew or sting and will not harm you. The only creatures that need to be scared of dragonflies are the insects they eat.

Myth: Woodchucks Eat Wood

How much wood would a woodchuck chuck if a woodchuck could chuck wood? It's fun to try and say this very quickly, but we know that woodchucks don't eat wood. They eat other plants, including grass, dandelions, and clover, but they don't eat trees.

Woodchucks snip plant stems with their four white front teeth (incisors), which never stop growing. They keep their teeth short by cutting plants to eat and grinding their teeth against each other.

Myth: Baby Birds Don't Eat Very Much

Has anyone ever told you that you eat like a bird? When someone says that, they usually mean that you don't have a big appetite and only eat a tiny bit of food.

However, birds, especially young birds, eat a LOT! A young bird that's still in the nest (nestling) and being fed by its parents may eat ten meals a day!

Myth: Owls Can Turn Their Head All the Way Around

Without moving your head, can you look to one side and then the other? Owls can't do this.

Owls have excellent eyesight, but their eyes are fixed in their head. They can only see straight ahead. If they want to see to the side or behind them, they must turn their head in that direction.

In order to move their head three-quarters of the way around, owls have 14 neck bones—twice as many as humans! They can almost, but not quite, turn their head all the way around.

Myth: Turtles Walk Away from Their Shells

Turtles have a top shell (carapace) and a bottom shell (plastron). Their top shell is mostly flattened ribs and a backbone. A turtle's body is attached to their ribs, just as our body is attached to our ribs.

A turtle can't walk away from its shell any more than you can walk away from your skeleton!

Myth: Snakes Are Slimy

Many people believe snakes are slimy. Have you ever touched a snake? If you have, you know that they are not slimy at all. A snake's body is covered with dry scales that overlap each other. The scales are made of the same material (keratin) as your fingernails and toenails.

Snakes use their scales to protect themselves and to help them grip the ground when they move.

Myth: Black Bears Hibernate

Black bears go to sleep in the fall and don't eat, drink, pee, or poop all winter. But they can wake up during the winter if they are disturbed and when they give birth. This kind of long sleep is called torpor.

True hibernators like woodchucks, bats, and jumping mice sleep so deeply they don't wake up until spring, even if disturbed.

Myth: Opossums Hang by Their Tails

You may see cartoons of opossums hanging upside down by their tail. While they do have a special tail that can grab onto branches and leaves (prehensile), opossums don't hang by it. They use it as well as their feet to help them hold on as they climb trees. They also use it to grasp leaves and other material to take to their den and use as bedding.

Myth: All Bees Die After They Sting

If a honey bee stings, the honey bee dies. Because of barbs, or hooks, on its tip, the honey bee's stinger gets caught in the animal it stings. When the bee flies away, its stinger and part of its body remain in the animal it has stung and the honeybee then dies.

Bumble bees, hornets, yellow jackets, and other wasps can sting over and over without hurting themselves because their stingers are smooth and are easily removed from whatever they have stung.

Myth: Your Face Will Freeze

Myths exist about people as well as animals. Sometimes children are told that if they make a funny face their face will freeze and stay that way forever. Of course, this isn't true!

For Creative Minds

Spiders Are Not Insects

Some people think spiders are insects, but they are not. Insects have six legs and three body parts. Spiders have eight legs and two body parts.

Can you tell which is an insect and which is a spider?

1
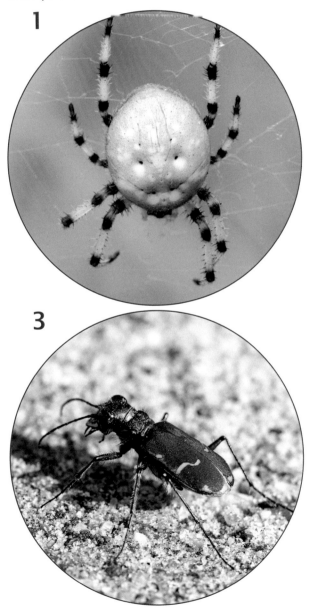

2

3

4

Answers: Insects: 2, 3 Spiders: 1, 4

Match the Animals to Their Defenses

All animals have adaptations to help them defend themselves. Can you match the animal to its defenses?

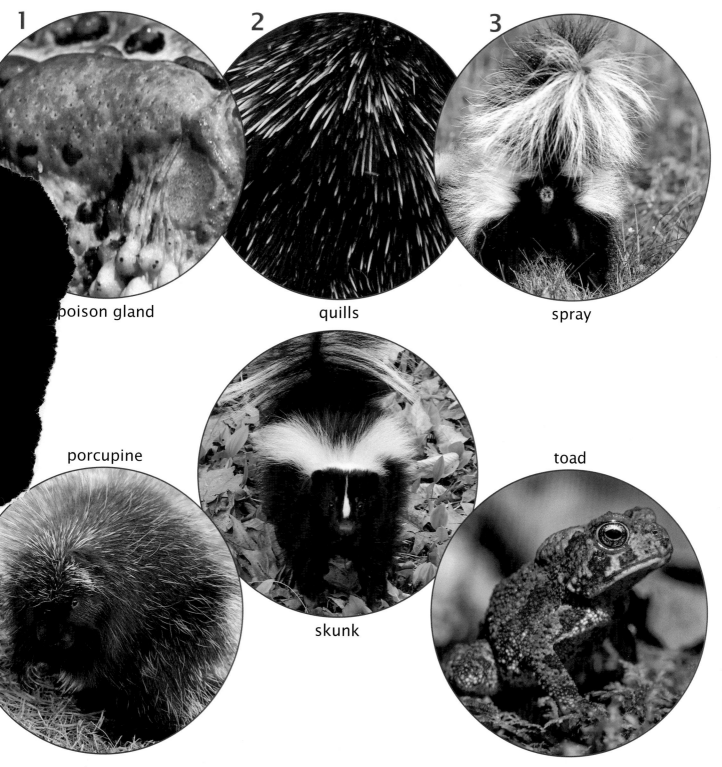

1 poison gland

2 quills

3 spray

porcupine

skunk

toad

Answers: 1-toad, 2-porcupine, 3-striped skunk

This book is dedicated to Pat Henderson, whose encouragement and unmitigated faith in me helped launch my writing career.—MH

Thanks to Sadie Brown for the use of her photo of her daughter, Lily Piper, making a funny face.

Thanks to the staff and volunteers at Cedar Bog Nature Preserve for verifying the information in this book.

Library of Congress Cataloging-in-Publication Data

Names: Holland, Mary, 1946- author.
Title: Animal myths / by Mary Holland.
Description: Mt. Pleasant, SC : Arbordale Publishing, LLC, [2023] |
   Includes bibliographical references.
Identifiers: LCCN 2022036976 (print) | LCCN 2022036977 (ebook) | ISBN
   9781643519814 (paperback) | ISBN 9781638170006 (interactive
   dual-language, read along) | ISBN 9781638170389 (epub) | ISBN
   9781638170198 (adobe pdf)
Subjects: LCSH: Animals--Miscellanea--Juvenile literature.
Classification: LCC QL49 .H684 2023 (print) | LCC QL49 (ebook) | DDC
   590--dc23/eng/20220804
LC record available at https://lccn.loc.gov/2022036976
LC ebook record available at https://lccn.loc.gov/2022036977

Translated into Spanish: *Mitos de Animales*
Spanish paperback ISBN: 9781638172611
Spanish ePub ISBN: 9781638172796
Spanish PDF ebook ISBN: 9781638172734
Dual-language read-along available online at www.fathomreads.com

English Lexile® Level: 820L

Bibliography

Holland, Mary. Naturally Curious: A Photographic Field Guide and Month-by-Month Journey through the
   Woods, and Marshes of New England. Second Edition. Trafalgar Square Books. North Pomfret, VT,
   Winner, National Outdoor Book Award.

Printed in the U
This product conforms to CPSIA 200

Arbordale Publishing, LL
Mt. Pleasant, SC 2946
www.ArbordalePublishing.co